Contents

Review

Background Reading

D0317492

2

The Picture in the Attic

Richard MacAndrew
Cathy Lawday
Series Editor: Rob Waring

NATIONAL
GEOGRAPHIC | CENGAGE

Australia • Brazil   United States

NATIONAL GEOGRAPHIC LEARNING | CENGAGE Learning·

Page Turners Reading Library
The Picture in the Attic
Richard MacAndrew
and Cathy Lawday

Publisher: Andrew Robinson

Executive Editor:
Sean Bermingham

Senior Development Editor:
Derek Mackrell

Assistant Editors:
Claire Tan, Sarah Tan

Story Editor: Julian Thomlinson

Series Development Editor:
Sue Leather

Director of Global Marketing:
Ian Martin

Content Project Manager:
Tan Jin Hock

Print Buyer: Susan Spencer

Layout Design and Illustrations:
Redbean Design Pte Ltd

Cover Illustration:
Eric Foenander

Photo Credits:
57 pkfawcett/iStockphoto,
59 Konstantin Sutyagin/
Shutterstock,
60 hairballusa/iStockphoto,
61 ell brown/Flickr

ISBN-13: 978-1-4240-1795-9

ISBN-10: 1-4240-1795-5

National Geographic Learning
20 Channel Center Street
Boston, MA 02210
USA

Cengage Learning is a leading provider of customized learning solutions with office locations around the globe, including Singapore, the United Kingdom, Australia, Mexico, Brazil, and Japan.

Cengage Learning products are represented in Canada by Nelson Education, Ltd.

Visit National Geographic Learning online at **ngl.cengage.com**

Visit our corporate website at **www.cengage.com**

Printed in the United States of America
4 5 6 7 16 15 14

People in the story

Emma and Charlie Taylor
a young couple who have just moved
into a new house

Carol Barton
their next-door neighbor

The story is set in Pangbourne, a small town in the UK.

Chapter 1

The new house

"Look at this!" said Emma excitedly. "I found it in the room at the top of the house. You know, the attic."

It was Emma and Charlie Taylor's first day in their new house. They'd only been married a few weeks, and this was their first home. In Emma's hands was an old picture of a young woman.

"It's good, isn't it?" she said. "I could put it on the wall. Over there by the window."

"Um . . . I don't know," said Charlie. "I think she looks a bit sad."

Emma looked at the picture again. "Yes. You're right. She does," said Emma. The woman in the picture was young, about 18 to 20 years old. She had green eyes and long brown hair. She had on a long green dress and a beautiful old watch. But she wasn't smiling.

"I'll leave it here on the floor for now," said Emma. "We can decide where to put it later."

Their new house was over 100 years old. It was on Horseshoe Road in Pangbourne, a small town about 80 kilometers from London. The house was very old and very dirty. But it was beautiful, and they loved it. Emma looked at the picture once more.

"I think it's a nice picture," she said. "Anyway, come on. There's lots of cleaning to do!"

They worked for three more hours. They washed and cleaned the kitchen and the living room. They put a table and some chairs in the kitchen, and they put away their books.

"I'm tired," said Charlie, looking at his watch. "It's seven o'clock. Why don't we go out for dinner?"

"Good idea," replied Emma.

They washed, put on some clean clothes, and walked out into the warm August evening. Emma and Charlie chose a restaurant by the river. They sat outside and ordered some food and drinks. They watched boats going up and down the river and talked about what they wanted to do to the house.

Charlie was 28. He had short blond hair and blue eyes. Emma was 29. She had blond hair, too. They had met at a party three years before. Charlie had been living in a flat in Pangbourne and working in London. Emma had been living in a small flat in London at that time, but she didn't like it. After they got married, Emma found a new job in Pangbourne so she could move away from London to be with Charlie. And then they found their beautiful house.

"I like Pangbourne," said Emma. "I'm going to be happy living here. I really didn't like London. It was too noisy and dirty. And too expensive."

"I hope we'll both be happy here," said Charlie.

"Yes, and I want to start our family here. It'll be a great place to bring up children," said Emma.

There was a silence. Emma could sense he had something to say. Something important.

"Well," he said at last, "one day. I know I said that one day I'd like children, but not just yet. We're still young. Let's wait a while. Maybe in a few years, okay?"

Emma smiled at him and put her hand on his. She knew this meant she'd have to wait for the children she had always wanted. "Sure. The important thing is to be with you."

Emma was quiet as they walked slowly back to their new home hand in hand.

That night, Emma had a dream. She was running through some trees. It was very dark in the trees, and something was behind her. She couldn't see what it was but it was making a noise. The noise got louder. Suddenly, Emma woke up. She really could hear a noise. She turned on a light and looked at her clock. It was 2:30.

"Listen!" she said to Charlie. "I can hear something!"

"Mmm . . . It's just a train," he answered.

"There aren't any trains at night!" she said.

"It's a cat then. Go back to sleep."

Emma sat up in bed.

"Charlie! Wake up! Listen. Please!"

There was a noise. It seemed like a kind of crying noise. Now Charlie could hear it, too. Charlie sat up, too.

"What is it?" asked Emma.

"I don't know," he answered.

They both listened carefully.

"It's coming from the attic!" said Charlie. "Did you leave the attic door open?"

"No, I didn't." answered Emma. "Did you leave the front door open?"

"Of course I didn't!" said Charlie angrily.

They listened. Then, suddenly, the noise stopped.

After a minute, Charlie got out of bed.

"I'm going to go and look," he said.

"Are you sure?" asked Emma. "Why not wait until morning?"

"I'm sure it's nothing," said Charlie.

Emma got out of bed.

"I'm coming, too," she said. "It's my house, too. If there is something there, I want to know what it is."

She took Charlie's hand. They walked slowly and carefully up the stairs to the attic. Emma stayed behind Charlie all the way. Charlie opened the door. Although he told himself he would find nothing, he felt the hairs on his arms standing up. Emma was holding one of his hands really tight.

Charlie opened the door slowly and looked inside. Emma stayed behind him.

"What's there, Charlie?" she asked nervously.

After a few seconds he said, "Nothing. Nothing at all. It's the same as this afternoon."

"Really? You're not joking, are you? We did hear something," Emma said.

"Really, there's nobody here," he said to Emma. "It must just be the house." He could feel Emma relax a little. She looked inside, too.

"Are you sure?" she asked again.

"Of course," said Charlie. "Old houses often make noises."

"Perhaps you're right," said Emma. But she wasn't as sure as Charlie. She didn't like the noises that came out of the attic.

They went back to bed and Emma turned out the light.

"I wonder if I'll hear them again," she thought to herself as she went back to sleep.

Chapter 2

A surprise for Emma

"I'll see you in a couple of days," Charlie said to Emma as he was leaving next morning.

"What?" she said sleepily. "You'll be gone for two days?"

"Yes," said Charlie, who wrote stories for a big London newspaper. "I told you. I'm working on a story up north in Newcastle. Not everyone can be a teacher like you and have long summer holidays." He smiled at her.

Suddenly, Emma's eyes were open, and she felt much more awake.

"Oh, I forgot. But Newcastle's miles away. It's the other end of the country. You don't mean you're leaving me alone here with the noises in the attic, do you?"

Charlie put a hand on Emma's hand.

"Don't be silly, Emma," he said. "Like I said last night, it's just this old house making funny noises. Nobody was there, remember?"

Emma didn't look happy. She didn't feel happy either.

"And I'm not well either," she said. "You know, I've got to see the doctor this morning."

"I'm sure it's nothing," said Charlie. "You said he wasn't worried at all when you saw him last week."

"Please, Charlie," said Emma. "Can't you call the office and say that you're not feeling well, that you're sick?"

Charlie just smiled at her.

"I'll see you in a couple of days. You'll be fine," he said again, trying to make her relax. He kissed the top of her head, picked up his bag, and left to walk to the station.

After last night, she didn't feel happy about being alone. "Perhaps if I keep myself busy, I'll feel better," she thought. "I have to see the doctor in the morning, and then there is more cleaning to do in the house, and so many boxes to put away." Quickly, she felt better.

"Hello, Mrs. Taylor. Do come in," said the doctor. Dr. Eliot was a short man with dark hair and glasses.

Emma went into the doctor's office and sat down. The doctor looked at his notes.

"You came to see me ten days ago," he said.

"That's right," said Emma. "I'm in my own house now. We moved in yesterday."

"That's nice," said the doctor. He put his notes on the table next to him. "Now then, you said you weren't feeling well in the mornings," he continued, "and we did some tests."

"That's right," said Emma.

"Well," said the doctor. He sat back in his chair and looked at Emma. "You're going to have a baby."

Emma put a hand up to her mouth. She didn't know what to say.

The doctor smiled at her.

"You didn't expect that, did you?" he said.

"No," said Emma. "I didn't."

"Well, if you're having a baby, it's quite normal to feel unwell in the morning," said the doctor. "It happens to a lot of women."

"Right," said Emma.

A lot of different thoughts were flying through her head.

"What's Charlie going to say?" "What about my new job?" "Will the baby be a boy or a girl?" "Why did this happen now?" "This isn't the right time for me to have a baby."

"Why don't you go home?" The doctor was speaking again. "You need time to think about this and talk to your husband. Then come back and see me sometime next week." He smiled again and put a hand on her arm. "Everything will be fine."

Emma left the doctor's and went to the shops to buy food. But she was thinking about the baby.

"What's Charlie going to say?" she asked herself again. "Last night he said he didn't want children for a long time." She had to tell him—but of course, he was away. "I can't tell him something like this on the phone," she thought. "I'll have to wait till he gets home. But how's he going to feel about becoming a father? And anyway, do I want this baby? I'm just starting a new job. I've just moved to a new town. This really is the wrong time for me to be having a baby."

These thoughts filled her mind until she got back home just after 11:30. As she walked toward their house, she saw a woman standing outside the front door of the next house. The woman was about 60 years old, with gray hair. She was wearing a red, blue, and green skirt with flowers on it, a white T-shirt, and lots of jewelry.

"Hello," said the woman to Emma. "I'm Carol. Carol Barton. Have you just moved in next door?"

"Yes, hello," said Emma. "It's nice to meet you. I'm Emma. Would you like a cup of coffee?" she asked. "It would be nice to talk to someone else and not worry about my problems for a few minutes," she thought. "And I should try and make some new friends in Pangbourne."

"Oh yes. Thank you," said Carol.

They went into the house.

"Come into the kitchen."

Emma made coffee and got out some cake. The two women sat at the table.

"Well, this is nice and clean!" said Carol. "It was very dirty when Miss Spencer lived here!"

"Yes," said Emma. "My husband, Charlie, was here yesterday, and we worked hard, but the bedrooms and bathroom are still very dirty."

"I'm happy there's someone living in this house now," said Carol. "After Miss Spencer died, nobody lived here. The house was empty for a long time."

"Did you know Miss Spencer?" asked Emma.

"Yes, I knew her," answered Carol. "She was a nice woman most of the time. But sometimes she was a bit strange."

"What do you mean?" asked Emma.

"Well, she lived alone here," said Carol. "And she had no other family. Sometimes she talked to herself. She just sat on a chair by the back door of her house and talked to herself."

"How strange," said Emma.

"And she often went to bed very late. Sometimes the light was on up in the attic till three or four o'clock in the morning."

Emma suddenly remembered the noises in the night and her face changed.

"Are you OK?" asked Carol. "What's the problem?"

Emma told Carol about the noises in the attic.

"You don't want to worry about that," said Carol. "It's just these old houses. They make lots of noises. Mostly at night."

"I hope you're right," thought Emma. "I hope you're right."

Chapter 3

More noises in the night

At about nine o'clock that evening, Emma was sitting in the living room drinking a cup of tea. She was thinking about cleaning the house and what she wanted to do the next day. One thing was to clean the windows in the kitchen and the living room. Emma used an old shirt to clean windows. She remembered that she had left her window-cleaning shirt in the attic.

"I'll just go up and get that," she thought. "Then it will be down here ready for tomorrow morning."

She started up the stairs quickly and confidently at first, but then, as she got higher, she started to slow down.

Suddenly, she began to feel a bit unsure. She didn't know why. Something felt very strange. Very, very strange.

On the first floor she stopped and listened. Her mouth felt dry. Her heart began to go faster. And a cold feeling of fear started slowly up the back of her neck.

"Why am I feeling so afraid?" she asked herself. "What's wrong with me? There's nothing up there. We looked last night."

One step at a time, she moved slowly up the stairs to the very top. She couldn't hear anything except her own heart getting louder and faster.

"Come on, Emma!" she said to herself. "Don't be silly. It's your house. There's nothing there. Don't be afraid. Just walk into the attic."

Slowly she reached forward and opened the door to the attic. She looked round the door into the room. There was a window on the right. It was open. "Who opened the window?" Emma asked herself. "Charlie, maybe."

Emma went into the room and reached over to close the window. Suddenly, there was a loud noise right outside the window. Emma jumped back, eyes wide open, and watched a bird fly away from a tree just near the window. "Silly me!" said Emma to herself. "It was just a bird." Then she said it again. "It was just a bird. Don't be stupid, Emma," actually speaking the words this time to make herself feel better. She wanted to tell herself that she wasn't being silly. But her heart was still going fast.

Feeling better, she began to look round the room. There was something strange about it. There were a lot of old books and papers behind the door, and a big old chair under the window. The window-cleaning shirt was on the back of the chair. The floor was clean, the window was clean, the books and papers were tidy. Then she realized why the room felt strange.

"That's it!" she thought. "Everywhere else in the house is very dirty. But this room isn't. It's clean. And I didn't even start to clean it yesterday. I don't understand it. Why is this room so clean and the others, not?"

She walked round the room. She looked behind the chair. There were some pretty dried flowers behind the chair. Emma picked them up. She looked round again with her back to the window. Her back felt cold as she noticed once again the clean and tidy room. "Why?" she thought. "Who did this? Not me. Not Charlie. And why this room? What was important about this room?" Again a cold feeling of fear moved up her back. She looked round the room. It was just a normal room but it did feel strange in some way. She couldn't say how, but something was not quite right. It was almost as if someone was living there.

She took the shirt off the back of the chair and quickly went back down to the kitchen. She put the flowers on the kitchen table. Thinking all the time about the attic, she made some coffee. Then she sat down and turned on the television. She had tried hard all day to forget the noises, but they kept coming back to her mind. "What were the noises? What was making them?"

She thought about the noises even as she fell asleep that evening.

◇◇◇

Suddenly, Emma woke up. The noise was back. The fear from earlier in the evening was suddenly back, too. She lay in bed for a time, wondering what to do. Staying in bed and doing nothing seemed a good idea. "I can go back to sleep and do something about it in the morning," she thought. But the noises continued.

Emma felt her heart begin to beat faster. She turned over in bed and pulled the covers over her head. She felt very scared, but she was also angry. After a few minutes she thought, "This can't go on. I'm going to have to do something. It's my house. I want to live here, and something or someone is trying to stop me. I don't want that to happen."

Slowly, she got out of bed. She looked round the bedroom in the half-dark. Her old hockey stick was next to the clothes cupboard. She picked it up and held it in front of her. If there was someone in the attic, she might need the hockey stick.

Little by little she opened the bedroom door and looked out. Was that something by the attic door? Or was it someone? It was someone. Emma could stand it no more. She screamed.

"Go away! This is my house, not yours," she shouted. She threw the stick towards the attic door and screamed again.

"Get out of my house!" But there was no reply. Nobody moved. Nothing happened. Feeling stronger, she said, "I'll call the police!" But again nothing happened.

Suddenly feeling frightened again, she ran back into the safety of her bedroom. She locked her bedroom door, jumped into bed, and pulled the covers up below her eyes. She was very afraid now. She started to cry. She couldn't take her eyes off her bedroom door. Then she thought of Charlie. "Charlie! Yes, of course, Charlie," she thought. "I can call Charlie. He'll know what to do."

She put a hand out to find the phone but knocked it onto the floor. She started to panic. It went under the bed. She couldn't find it. Making small crying noises, she put a hand out and reached around on the floor for the phone. Finally, she found it.

She called Charlie's number.

"Uh? Hello," answered Charlie sleepily.

"Charlie. It's me."

"Emma? What time is it?" asked Charlie. Then, "Emma! It's the middle of the night!"

"Charlie. There . . . there were noises in the attic again. Earlier this evening and . . . and again just now," said Emma. She couldn't get the words out fast enough. "And this time I saw something. I saw something. Someone. I saw someone."

"What did you see?" asked Charlie. He didn't sound fully awake yet.

"I think it was someone's foot," said Emma. "Someone in a green dress."

"Maybe it was that woman from the picture," Charlie laughed.

"Charlie! Don't laugh at me!" said Emma, angry now. "I'm telling you. I saw someone."

Charlie didn't speak for a few moments. Then he said, "Emma, was the light on?"

"No," she replied. "No, it wasn't."

"Well, maybe you just thought you saw someone. It was dark. Things look different in the dark."

"Charlie, I saw someone! Believe me! I saw someone. Here, at home, in our home," said Emma almost crying. "I want you to come back. I need you here. I don't feel safe."

"Emma, it's the middle of the night," said Charlie. "And I'm miles away in Newcastle. You're not thinking straight. Anyway I'm working tomorrow. I've got to see someone at 8:30. Now I'm sure you thought you saw someone, but I really don't think you did. I really don't think you need to worry. Go back to sleep, and everything will be fine in the morning."

There was silence. Emma took the phone away from her ear and looked at it. She was shocked. Charlie didn't believe her! She put the phone back to her ear.

"I'm sure everything will be fine," he said again. "Look, I'll talk to you in the morning . . ."

"But . . ." she began.

"Goodnight, Emma."

"Night, Charlie," said Emma very quietly.

She turned off the phone, then sat up and put the light on. At first she felt surprised at Charlie but then she began to feel angry. "Why didn't he believe me? He's my husband. He should believe me," she said to herself. "He should help me when I need him. I mean, he's staying in a nice hotel and I'm here in a house that makes strange noises And he won't even come back early to be with me. He just doesn't seem to care."

Emma listened again for the noise, but it was not there now. The house was quiet. She started to feel better. She felt stronger, too. She wanted to find out about who was making the noise. She wanted to find out who the person was.

She got out of bed and slowly opened her bedroom door again. There was nothing there. It was still quiet. "Maybe too quiet," she thought. Slowly, she walked up the stairs to the attic. There was nothing there either. She saw nobody. "Maybe Charlie was right," she thought. "Maybe it was my imagination."

She looked around the attic. "It's very cold in here," she thought. She looked at the window, but it wasn't open.

"Maybe I didn't see anything," said Emma to herself. "Charlie was right. It's an old house and it makes noises. Old houses do make noises. The lights were off and I thought I saw something but I didn't really. It's very easy to think you see something in the dark. Maybe I'm just feeling strange because I'm having a baby. The doctor said women who are expecting babies sometimes do strange things. I've read about that, too. Maybe I'm feeling a bit scared because I'm expecting a baby. Maybe that's why I think I'm hearing things and seeing things. That must be the answer."

Emma went back to her bedroom and got into bed. She felt better now that she thought Charlie might be right. She felt a little silly. She thought, "I can ring him in the morning and say I'm sorry for waking him up. He must be angry with me."

Emma tried to go to sleep but couldn't. She couldn't stop thinking about the attic and the noises. And the foot. "But, maybe I'm right. Maybe there is something in the attic." It was her last thought before she went to sleep.

Chapter 4

What's really happening?

When Emma woke the next morning it was a beautiful day. Maybe Charlie was right. Maybe she was imagining things. She went downstairs.

Emma finished her breakfast and then decided to go for a walk. She left her coffee cup on the kitchen table, locked her front door, and went out into the warm sun. "I'll wash it up when I get back," she thought.

She walked along the river, thinking about her baby. "It really isn't a good time to have a baby," she thought. She didn't really know anyone in Pangbourne—except Charlie. She worried about starting her new job, and the head teacher at her new school would be annoyed if she took time off to have the baby. It wasn't a good time.

After an hour she turned back. On the way back home she thought about the attic and the noises. "Charlie was right," she decided. "It was too dark to see anything last night. And the house is old; old houses do make noises. I must call him and say sorry."

Emma arrived back at the house at about 11 o'clock. Walking into the kitchen, she stopped. Her mouth fell open. "Oh no!" she said. "What happened?" The coffee cup she left on the table, was broken into pieces. "How did that happen?" She asked herself. "I left it on the table. And I locked the door!"

At first, Emma thought she was imagining things, but no, it really was broken. She tried hard to keep control. She looked round the room. Everything else seemed okay. She tried to think of a reason. "Why did the cup break? It must have just broken by itself," she thought. "Cups sometimes do just break. It's unusual but it happens."

She looked round the room again. "Everything's OK," she told herself. "Nothing's wrong."

Just then there was a loud noise, a breaking sound behind her. Emma jumped. She quickly looked round. "Who is that?" she screamed as she turned around quickly. And then she saw it. Her kitchen window was broken from the top to the bottom.

"How did that happen?" she asked herself. She could feel the fear from last night starting again: her heart beating faster. "Is this real?" she asked herself. "What's happening in this house?" She looked hard at the window. But the window started to change.

Suddenly, there was another longer breaking sound. The window changed completely. It was impossible to see through it; there were now little breaks all over it.

"Who's doing this?" she screamed. "Why are you doing this? Leave me alone. Leave me and my baby alone! Get out of my house."

And then the window broke in pieces all over the floor.

Emma screamed and ran to the phone.

"Charlie! Charlie!" she cried. "It's terrible. It's terrible."

"What's terrible?" asked Charlie.

Emma told him about the cup and the window.

"Look, Emma," said Charlie. "Cups and windows do break. You just said so yourself. Maybe there were some children outside. Maybe they threw a stone at the window."

"No, Charlie. I didn't see anyone."

"Well," Charlie almost sounded angry. "I'm in a meeting right now. And there's nothing I can do about it from here. I'm coming back to Pangbourne tonight. I'll see you then. OK?"

"But Charlie, I need . . ." she said.

"Emma!" he said angrily. "I told you. I'm in a meeting. I'll see you tonight."

"OK."

Emma started to cry quietly to herself.

"What is happening? Charlie is angry with me," she worried. "I don't want him to be angry with me because I need to tell him about the baby. But these things are really happening. And they aren't normal. Something very strange is happening, but Charlie won't believe it. He doesn't believe me." She felt very alone. She touched her stomach and said to her baby. "Don't worry, everything's going to be alright."

Just then there was a noise at the door. Emma jumped.

"Go away!" she shouted. "Get away from my house!"

"Hello?" she heard a voice say. "Emma, is that you?" Then she realized it was Carol's voice.

Emma dried her eyes and opened the door.

Carol took one look at Emma.

"Emma. What's wrong?" she asked.

"I don't know," began Emma and she started to cry again. "I don't know."

Carol put her arms round Emma and held her.

"I can't tell Carol about this," Emma thought. "I don't know her at all. Charlie doesn't believe me so I'm sure Carol won't."

But then she couldn't control herself any longer. She told Carol everything. She told her about the noises in the attic and about the person she thought she saw. She showed her the broken cup and the broken window.

"Did you hear anything next door?" asked Emma.

"No," said Carol, "I didn't. But the walls are thick."

She put a hand on Emma's arm.

"Come on," she said. "Let's go in the kitchen and I'll make you a cup of coffee."

Carol picked up the broken glass and made them both a cup of coffee. They sat at the kitchen table, and Carol changed the subject and talked to Emma about life in Pangbourne. After a few minutes she put a hand on Emma's arm and said, "There! You're looking a bit better now."

"Thank you," said Emma. "I feel better."

"When are you having the baby?" asked Carol

Emma's mouth fell open, and then she laughed.

"How do you know?" she asked.

"I was a doctor for 20 years," said Carol. "Women often cry a lot and do strange things when they're having a baby. I once knew a woman who ate newspaper."

Emma smiled and almost laughed again. "Well, yes, I am having a baby," she said, "but the doctor only told me yesterday morning, and Charlie, my husband, doesn't know yet. He's away on business. He's coming home this evening and I'm going to tell him then."

"Well, that's great," said Carol. "I hope you'll be very happy."

"So do I," said Emma sounding a bit worried. "But this is really the wrong time for me to have a baby," she continued. "I've known Charlie for three years, but we haven't really decided when we want children. I'm living in a new town and I've got a new job. We've just moved into this house, and strange things are going on. It's all a bit much for me."

Carol put a hand on Emma's arm again. She looked at her carefully and said, "It's never a good time to have a baby. You just need to talk to Charlie. And as for the noises, you don't need to worry about them either."

"What do you mean?" asked Emma.

"Well, things can seem strange when you find out you're having a baby. But these houses do make strange noises. I know mine does. And cups and windows do break."

She smiled at Emma.

"Don't make things more important than they are!" continued Carol. "It's only an old house and a broken cup."

Emma smiled back at Carol. She was beginning to like her.

"Thank you," she said and dried her eyes again. "I think I just needed someone to tell me that. I wish Charlie was here."

Then a thought came to her.

"Carol, you said Miss Spencer lived here before me. What else do you know about her?"

"Well, she lived here for over 60 or 70 years."

"60 or 70 years!" said Emma. "That's a long time."

"Yes. She came here with her father in 1938, I think it was. She was about 16 years old then. Her father died some time ago. I never knew him. I only came here about six years ago."

"She never got married then?" asked Emma.

"No. She told me she had a boyfriend once. He was an American soldier. He was fighting in the Second World War. But he died in 1945, in France. And she never wanted another boyfriend. She was a nice woman, but she was a bit sad and a bit strange."

"Did anyone live here with her?" asked Emma.

"No, not after her father died," answered Carol. "Just Miss Spencer. But now you're here! Do you like it?"

"Yes, I love the house! But I don't like the strange noises," said Emma laughing. She thought for a moment and said, "Carol, I want to show you something." She went to get the picture from the next room. "Look at this picture. I found it in the attic," she said.

Carol smiled when she saw it. "I see she hasn't left then," she said and laughed.

"What do you mean?" asked Emma.

"That's Miss Spencer," said Carol. "Her picture's here even if she's gone."

After Carol left, Emma felt better. She went into the kitchen and washed up the cups. She went back to the living room, put on some music, and sat down.

"I'm sure Carol's right about my baby," she thought. She put a hand on her stomach and smiled to herself. "I need to wait and talk to Charlie. She's probably right about the noises, too. Nothing really strange has happened. It's just my mind. And the fact that I'm expecting a baby. Old houses make noises. I only thought I saw someone—I wasn't absolutely sure; cups break, so do windows. And Charlie will be back this evening so everything will be alright. I hope he's not too angry with me."

There was a photo of Charlie and her on a small table near the window. She looked at the photo and smiled. The smile soon turned to worry. "What is Charlie going to say when I tell him I'm having a baby? Will he be all right about it?" she thought. "I think so but I don't know for certain." The other night had worried her. She pulled her legs up and put her arms round them. She didn't want to think about any other possibilities right now.

Emma looked round the room, deciding what to do next. Perhaps she should go up to the attic just to show herself that everything was okay and that nothing strange was happening.

"Come on, Emma!" she said to herself. "Show yourself that it's just an old house making a few noises."

She walked up the stairs, not so slowly this time. She opened the door and started into the room, but suddenly she stopped. Her mouth fell open in complete surprise. The books and papers were not behind the door any more. They were all over the floor. Some of the books were open. Papers were everywhere.

Emma looked round the room. "What's happened?" she asked herself.

She noticed the window was open, again.

"Maybe I left it open by mistake," she thought, "and the wind blew everything around the room."

Outside it was a warm day and not windy but here in the attic it was cold. Emma noticed this, too, and wondered about it.

She walked into the room a little way. One of the papers started to move, then another, then another. One by one they started to fly around in the air.

"My God!" thought Emma. "What's happening?"

One of the books started to open and close. Then another. Emma's eyes opened wide.

"Stop!" she shouted "Stop!" She didn't know what to do. She didn't know if she should stay or run.

The papers started to fly around the room. Emma caught one as it flew past. She tried to catch another but almost fell as she reached for it.

A book flew across the room into the wall, then another one. Emma screamed and ran to a corner of the room. She put her arms over her stomach. "My baby," she thought. "What will happen if a book hits the baby?"

The room suddenly got colder. Then everything stopped moving.

Emma just stood, her eyes wide open, her arms over her stomach. Nothing moved. Slowly, Emma put her hands down and looked round the room.

She looked at the papers all over the floor. They were letters. Without thinking, she picked one up. Then she went round the room picking up all the letters. She didn't know what to do. She couldn't think. She put the books back behind the door. She closed the window. She took the letters down to the kitchen and put them on the table.

She sat down and looked out of the window. Outside it was a beautiful sunny day. "Not windy at all," she thought. "How could the letters and books fly around the room like that?" She sat at the kitchen table, thoughts flying around inside her head.

Time passed. The house stayed quiet. Emma felt tired, sad, and alone. She went into the living room and sat down in one of the big armchairs. She was so tired, she wanted to sleep. "What is happening in my home?" She had a terrible thought. "Is there a ghost in the house? Is it Miss Spencer's ghost?"

Then, just before she went to sleep, she thought, "I can't go on like this. This has to stop."

Chapter 5

My dear Alice . . .

Emma woke up an hour or two later. She went into the kitchen and saw all the papers from the attic on the kitchen table. She remembered that they were letters. From somewhere a thought came to her that they might be important.

She took one and read it. It began "My dear Alice." The name at the bottom was George. She picked up another one. It was another letter from George to Alice. She put all the papers together. They were all letters, all from George to Alice. There were 36 of them. She went through them, looking at the dates. They were all from 1944 or 1945. She found the first one: 20th June 1944. Then she found the next, and the next, through to the last one on 27th March 1945. Then she read the first one. It was a love letter from George to Alice.

"Alice must be Miss Spencer," thought Emma. "And George must be her American boyfriend." She finished reading the letter. But it didn't feel right. "I really shouldn't read someone else's love letters," she said to herself. And she put them down without reading any more.

At seven o'clock Charlie arrived. He looked tired after his long journey home.

"Charlie!" Emma ran toward him and put her arms around him. Charlie put his bag down on a chair. "It's been terrible," started Emma. Charlie didn't have time to sit down. "Not just the glass and the window I told you about," she continued. "But I went into the attic again and . . ."

Emma told him again about the cup and the window and then about the books and papers in the attic.

"I'll go and have a look," said Charlie.

"There's nothing to see," said Emma. "I put everything back."

Charlie looked at her.

"Charlie! You do believe me, don't you?"

"Emma," began Charlie. "Old houses make noises, and cups and windows do break but books and papers don't fly around rooms. And I'm quite tired. I want to believe you but . . ."

This was too much for Emma. She picked up Charlie's bag and threw it at him angrily. "You don't believe me, do you?" she shouted. "You think I'm crazy. Well, take your bag and go and stay in a hotel. If you don't believe me, I don't want to talk to you. We've only been married a few weeks, and already you don't trust me."

"Emma . . . ," began Charlie.

"It all happened, Charlie," shouted Emma.

"Emma . . . ," began Charlie again.

"Come back when you believe me," said Emma angrily.

Charlie stood and waited.

"Go away!" Emma screamed. She turned around and walked into the kitchen. A moment or two later she heard the front door close. She put her head in her hands and started to cry.

A few minutes later Emma stopped crying. "I hate this house," she thought to herself. "I hate this house, this place; I hate Pangbourne. I'm going to have to leave."

Then she thought about Charlie. "Oh, why did I get angry with him? I have to tell him about the baby." She made herself a cup of tea and sat there for hours just worrying. And crying.

After a while, she dried her eyes and looked round the room, wondering what to do now. She started to make a cup of tea and then noticed the letters from George to Alice. She read the first one again and then decided to read them all. It was clear that George and Alice were very much in love. Finally, Emma came to the last letter. She read it, and then she read it again.

27th March 1945

My dear Alice,

I got your letter this morning. How happy I am! You say you are scared. I can understand that. But I love you very much. I am in France now, and far away from you, but I will be home soon. Then we can get married; you can have the baby; and we can become a happy family. I cannot wait to be a husband and a father. Don't tell your father. Don't tell anyone yet. First, let's get married. Wait for me.

With all my love,

George

"What was this about Miss Spencer and a baby?" wondered Emma. "Carol didn't say anything about Miss Spencer having a child. George died in the war. Miss Spencer lived here in this house for 60 years. But what happened to the baby? Perhaps Miss Spencer had the baby and it was taken away because she wasn't married. Maybe she lost the baby."

Suddenly, Emma put a hand on her front. She thought about her baby. "I can't let anything happen to my baby."

She thought about Charlie. She and Charlie were married—unlike George and Alice. And for George and Alice in 1945, it was very different. In 1945, life was difficult if you had a baby but you weren't married. "Poor Miss Spencer," she thought. "First, she found out she was having a baby. How did she feel about that? Then George told her he wanted to get married. But then he died. What did Miss Spencer feel like when she heard that news?"

Then Emma thought about Charlie. She was angry with him. Very angry. "But was he angry with me?" she wondered. "Are we going to be OK? And what about the baby?" She needed to tell him about the baby. She badly needed to talk to him—but not now.

Suddenly, she felt tired again. It was only ten o'clock but she decided to go to bed. Perhaps things would seem better in the morning.

But that night things got much worse.

Chapter 6

A terrible crying

"Help us! Help us!"

Suddenly, Emma was awake. Her eyes were wide open. "What was that?" she thought. "A voice? Or nothing?" Then she remembered the words of Carol and Charlie. "I must be imagining things again." She thought and tried to go back to sleep. Feeling cold, she pulled the covers higher and tried to get warm. She put her arms round her stomach. Lying on her side, she couldn't see behind her.

Then she heard a sound. She didn't want to look. But she had to.

She turned to see what was making the noise. There was a woman standing by the bed. She had long gray hair and was wearing a green dress. She was looking straight at Emma.

Emma was so scared she couldn't speak. She couldn't move. She couldn't do anything. The woman's mouth moved. It made a small sound, but Emma couldn't hear the words. Emma watched. She couldn't take her eyes away. She felt as if her body couldn't move, as if it were frozen.

"Help us! Help us!" she thought the woman was saying.

Then the woman turned and Emma watched her. The woman moved away. Emma's eyes were wide open in surprise. The woman didn't open the door. She seemed to move up to it and then through it.

"My God," thought Emma, "she's a ghost! A ghost in my house!" At first she wanted to run away. Then she realized that the ghost wanted something. She wanted Emma's help.

Suddenly, Emma felt she could move again.

She looked to her left, then to her right. She didn't know what to do. She thought, "Who is the woman? Is she really a ghost? Or is it my mind again? But maybe she is real. If so, what does she want? Why is she here?"

Emma threw off the covers and turned on the light. "What am I going to do? I can't call Charlie because he doesn't believe me. The police won't believe me either."

Suddenly, everything seemed too much for her. She screamed.

Just then there was a loud noise from the front door.

Emma screamed again. She threw open the bedroom door and shouted: "Go away! Go away! Leave me alone!"

Then she heard Charlie's voice from outside. "Emma," he was calling, "open the door. I can't do this. I have to talk to you."

Emma ran down to the front door in her night clothes. Her hair was all over the place. She threw open the door and half cried, half shouted at Charlie, "What do you want? I need help. This house . . ."

"Emma," Charlie stopped her speaking. "We can't stay . . ."

There was a loud noise from the attic. Then another. Then a lot of noises all together.

"Charlie!" shouted Emma, and threw herself into his arms.

"What on earth was that?" asked Charlie. His face was white. His eyes were wide open. He looked up the stairs. There were more loud noises.

"See? Now do you believe me?" she said. "I wasn't making up stories. I wasn't lying."

Suddenly, the front door closed loudly behind them. They both jumped and then ran for the stairs. They stopped outside the bedroom and looked at each other.

"What's happening, Emma?" asked Charlie.

"Charlie, listen to me. I know you're not going to believe me, but I think it's a ghost," she replied.

"A ghost?!" replied Charlie. He looked at her for a long time. "It can't be. There are no such things as ghosts! Now you're just being silly."

"Well, I saw her!" she shouted angrily at him. "Just five minutes ago. She was by my bed. The ghost has been making the noise and breaking things. The ghost is making those noises in the attic right now!" She looked into Charlie's eyes. She wanted him to believe her.

"But . . ." Charlie started, "but there aren't any such things as ghosts!"

"Well, if you don't believe me, you go into the attic and show me I'm wrong," she said angrily.

Suddenly, Charlie realized that Emma was serious. "Really? A . . . ghost?" he asked. "What's a ghost doing in this house?"

"I think it's something to do with Miss Spencer—she lived here before me—and her baby," Emma replied.

"What are you talking about?" asked Charlie.

There was another loud noise from the attic and the sound of breaking glass.

Emma held Charlie's arm again. She carried on with the story.

"I found some letters. In 1945, Miss Spencer was having a baby. But Carol, the woman next door, told me Miss Spencer never married and she didn't have any other family."

"So?" asked Charlie.

"So I don't know," explained Emma, "but I think it's important."

There was more noise from the attic and then a kind of crying sound.

"What's that sound?" asked Charlie.

Emma put a hand to her mouth.

"Let's go and see," she said.

"We can't," said Charlie.

"We must," said Emma. "I have to know."

Slowly, they climbed the stairs to the attic. They held each other's hand nervously. As they got nearer the attic door, they could hear more noises. Then they heard something louder. It was the sound of breaking wood. Then more breaking glass. Then silence.

"You first, Charlie," said Emma.

"What?"

"Charlie!" said Emma. "You go first. It can't be a ghost, remember?"

"OK, OK," he said.

Charlie continued up the stairs. Slowly he opened the door and looked into the room. The window was open and broken. The books were everywhere again: all over the floor, some open, some in pieces, some with pages missing. The chair was broken, one leg in the middle of the room, the rest of the chair in a corner.

Charlie's mouth fell open. "What's happening?" he asked.

Then the window started to move backward and forward. Some bits of glass fell out onto the floor; other bits flew across the room, just missing Emma and Charlie.

"What the . . . ?" said Charlie in surprise.

Emma screamed and threw herself behind the door. She put her arms over her stomach to protect herself and her baby.

One of the books started opening and closing, then another. Then one flew across the room. The wood of the chair, already broken, started to move as if someone was hitting it. Pieces of wood flew off all round the room. The broken chair leg rose up in the air and flew at Charlie. It only just missed his head and hit the wall behind him with a loud noise.

"Emma!" shouted Charlie, but he couldn't say anymore as a book hit him straight in the face. His hands went up to his face as the book fell to the floor. Then, as suddenly as it had started, everything went quiet again. Emma started to run out of the door. "I'm getting out of here!" she said. But Charlie stopped her.

"No, wait!" he said.

Emma looked at Charlie.

"Charlie, let's go. Now!" she said angrily. "I don't like it in here."

But he wasn't moving. Emma looked at him.

"Charlie, what's wrong?" Emma asked. "What are you doing?"

Charlie put up a hand. He was listening to something.

"Shh! I can hear something," he said, putting his head on one side.

They both listened.

"Over there," said Emma. "By the wall."

They both went over to the wall, slowly and carefully. Emma put a hand on the wall. Then she put her ear to the wall and listened. Suddenly, she jumped back, her face white, her hand to her mouth.

"What is it?" asked Charlie.

Emma didn't speak so Charlie listened to the wall. Then he stood up, a strange look on his face.

"It sounds like a baby, doesn't it?" he said.

"Yes," said Emma quietly.

"But that's impossible," said Charlie.

"Yes," said Emma.

"You stay here a moment," he said to Emma.

Charlie went downstairs and came back with a knife. He put the knife into the wall and turned it. Pieces of stone came out. Then a whole stone. Then a second stone, and a third. It was slow work.

The crying got louder and louder. "Charlie, it's getting louder. Quick, let's get it out."

Charlie worked at the wall for about half an hour. Emma helped by moving the stones across to the other side of the room. They didn't speak. The room was quiet; there was just the sound of knife on stone.

Finally, Charlie found an opening, a hole inside the wall. He looked inside. "There's something here," he said quietly.

"What is it?" asked Emma. She came across the room and looked into the hole with him.

"I don't know," replied Charlie. "It looks like some old clothes."

Charlie put his hand into the hole. He took out the pieces of old clothes.

"I think there's something inside," he said.

He put the clothes on the floor and started to open them.

"There is something inside," he said. Emma watched as he pulled away the last of the clothes.

"Oh no!" Emma's hand went to her mouth.

"Quickly!" said Charlie. "Go and call the police!"

On the floor in front of them was a small baby.

The bones of a small dead baby.

Chapter 7

A few days later

A few days later, Charlie and Emma were standing outside the front door of St. Mary's Church in Pangbourne. They were standing next to a fresh hole in the ground. They saw Carol Barton coming towards them.

Emma introduced Charlie to Carol.

Charlie smiled at Carol. Then he looked down at the hole in the ground and said to Emma, "So Miss Spencer's baby boy is now back beside his mother. They're together again."

"I'm still not sure I understand the whole story," said Carol.

"When Alice Spencer died," explained Emma, "they brought her body here to St. Mary's Church, but of course her baby was still in the wall in our house."

"I see," said Carol.

"Do you think there'll be any more noises at night?" Charlie asked Emma.

"I'm sure there won't," she said.

"So why did Miss Spencer's ghost come to you?" Carol asked.

"I don't know," Emma said. "But that night—the night we found the baby—I think Miss Spencer was angry—angry that we were in her house and angry that she and her baby were not together. Now they're together again, she won't be angry anymore."

Emma turned and looked up at Charlie.

"By the way, the other night you started to say something. What was it?"

A strange look came over Charlie's face, but then he smiled quickly.

"Nothing really," he said. "I came to say sorry. Sorry that I didn't believe you." Emma looked at Charlie. Then Carol asked, "Are the police sure it was her baby?"

"Yes," said Emma. "The scientists got DNA from the baby's body and from the envelope that the letter was in. George was the father, and they're almost certain Alice Spencer was the mother."

"The scientists could also tell that the baby never lived. It died before it was even born," added Charlie.

Emma spoke again, "And Miss Spencer wasn't married. So, when the baby was born dead, she put it in the wall in the attic. And that's why the attic was clean."

"What do you mean it was clean?" asked Carol.

"You know, when we moved into the house, everywhere was very dirty. But the attic was quite clean and tidy," said Emma. "When Miss Spencer lived there, she sat in the attic, read her love letters, and could be near her baby. That's why the attic light was on so late at night."

"I see," said Carol.

"And now Alice Spencer's baby boy is with his mother again," she said. "I'm sure that's what she wants."

"That's what who wants?" asked Carol.

"Everyone really," said Emma and smiled at Charlie.

Carol said good-bye and left to walk home. Emma looked at Charlie. He didn't know about their baby yet, and she really needed to tell him. Straight after finding Miss Spencer's baby, Charlie had gone away again on business. There was no time to tell him about her visit to the doctor. This was his first day back in Pangbourne and Emma was worried about telling him. But this seemed like a good moment.

Charlie put his arm round Emma.

"You know, I think we're going to be very happy here. Now that you're here in Pangbourne," he said.

"I know we are," she said. "All of us: you, me, and the baby."

"Whose baby?" said Charlie. "What are you talking about? Miss Spencer's baby?"

Emma smiled. "No, silly." Emma was looking at her hands and playing with her fingers. "I went to the doctor's last week." Then she looked up at Charlie. "We're going to have a baby."

Charlie put his arms round her and said, "Really? That's wonderful news. But why didn't you tell me before?"

Emma looked up at him. "The last few days were a bit strange," she said. "I wanted to tell you but . . ."

"That's wonderful," he said and pulled her close again.

"But Charlie . . . ," she started nervously. "The other night you said you didn't want children for a long time."

Charlie looked at her and said, "I know. But I saw how you felt the other night when I was asking you to wait. I realized how important it is to you to have children. Miss Spencer didn't get the chance to have her baby. I'm not going to give up our chance."

"Oh, Charlie, I do love you," said Emma.

"What shall we call him?" asked Charlie.

"Her!" she replied playfully. They both laughed. He kissed her and lifted her into the air.

"Hey, be careful of our little girl!" she said, laughing.

Review: Chapters 1–4

A. Match the characters in the story with their descriptions.

1. the Taylors' neighbor
2. Emma's doctor
3. a young newly wed reporter
4. the previous owner of the house
5. a young newly wed teacher

a. Emma Taylor
b. Charlie Taylor
c. Miss Spencer
d. Dr. Eliot
e. Carol Barton

B. Choose the best answer for each question.

1. Charlie and Emma find a picture of . . .

   a. a young woman.

   b. the house.

   c. the town.

2. Their first night in the house they hear a noise in . . .

   a. the kitchen.

   b. the attic.

   c. the living room.

3. When she finds out Charlie is going to Newcastle, Emma . . .

   a. wants to go too.

   b. feels happy for him.

   c. wants him to stay at home.

4. At the doctor's Emma finds out . . .

   a. she must have some tests.

   b. she is very well.

   c. she is having a baby.

5. Emma thinks . . .

   a. Charlie opened the window in the attic.

   b. the window in the attic came open in the wind.

   c. the bird somehow opened the window in the attic.

6. When Emma rings Charlie in the middle of the night, he . . .

   a. gets angry with her.

   b. is very worried about the noises.

   c. doesn't think there is a problem.

7. Emma is worried because . . .

   a. Carol broke the window when she was out.

   b. Charlie doesn't believe she's hearing noises.

   c. she doesn't know anything about Miss Spencer.

8. What did Emma take downstairs from the attic?

   a. some books

   b. some letters

   c. some flowers

C. Complete the paragraph with the correct form of the verbs in the box.

look	see	be	get	be	hear	tell	find
think	go	find	hear	call	get	break	

On Charlie and Emma's first night in their new house they heard strange noises from upstairs. They **1.** _____ up and **2.** _____ in the attic but they **3.** _____ nothing there. The next night Emma **4.** _____ at home on her own and she **5.** _____ more noises. She also **6.** _____ she **7.** _____ someone outside her bedroom door. She **8.** _____ Charlie but he **9.** _____ her not to worry. The following morning Emma **10.** _____ for a walk. When she **11.** _____ back to the house, she **12.** _____ a broken glass on the kitchen table and while she **13.** _____ in the kitchen the window **14.** _____.

D. Fill in the correct words. What is the hidden word? _____ .

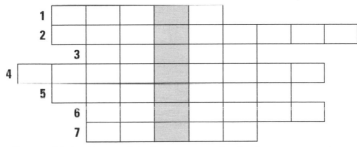

1. Emma thinks there might be a _____ in the house.

2. Emma was _____ when the doctor said she was having a baby.

3. Emma and Charlie had to _____ the house when they moved in.

4. Emma thought London was noisy, dirty, and _____.

5. Emma is a _____.

6. Charlie can't come straight back to Pangbourne because he has a _____.

7. Carol tells Emma not to _____.

Review: Chapters 5–7

A. Number these events in the order they happened.

Emma and Charlie hear loud noises in the attic. _____

Emma reads the letters from George to Miss Spencer. _____

Emma and Charlie hear noises in the attic wall. _____

Emma sees a woman standing by her bed. _____

Emma tells Charlie she is going to have a baby. _____

Emma and Charlie find the bones of a small dead baby. _____

The police think it was probably Miss Spencer's baby. _____

B. Read each statement and circle whether it is true (T) or false (F).

1 Emma told Charlie to go away because he didn't believe her.   T / F

2. Emma thought the woman by her bed was asking for help.   T / F

3. Emma and Charlie think they can hear a bird in the wall.   T / F

4. Charlie makes a hole in the wall.   T / F

5. Emma and Charlie go to the police station.   T / F

6. The bones of the dead baby are put next to its mother.   T / F

C. Complete this letter from Emma to her friend. Use words from the box. Put one word in each space.

scared	flying	actually	sad	bones
guess	crying	nervous	standing	

And then I woke up in the middle of the night and there was a woman standing by my bed. I was so 1. _____ I jumped out of bed and started screaming. Charlie came back just then. And there was a lot of noise from the attic. He had to believe me then! He 2. _____ started to look 3. _____.
Well, we went up to the attic and everything was 4. _____ around the room. A book hit Charlie in the face. Then there was this 5. _____ noise from the wall. Charlie made a hole in the wall and you'll never 6. _____ what we found there. The 7. _____ of a dead baby. It was so 8. _____.
Of course we had to call the police and . . .

D. Complete each sentence with a word beginning with "b."

1. Charlie was away on b_____.

2. George was Miss Spencer's b_____.

3. Emma threw Charlie's b_____ at him.

4. Emma was angry because Charlie didn't b_____ her.

5. Miss Spencer told George she was going to have his b_____.

6. Emma and Charlie found some b_____ in the wall.

7. When they went into the attic, the chair was b_____.

Answer Key

Chapters 1–4

A:
1. e;   **2.** d;   **3.** b;   **4.** c;   **5.** a.

B:
1. a;   **2.** b;   **3.** c;   **4.** c;   **5.** a;   **6.** c;   **7.** b;   **8.** b.

C:
1. got;   **2.** looked;   **3.** found;   **4.** was;   **5.** heard;   **6.** thought;   **7.** saw;
8. called;   **9.** told;   **10.** went;   **11.** got;   **12.** found;   **13.** was;   **14.** broke.

D:
1. ghost;   **2.** surprised;   **3.** clean;   **4.** expensive;   **5.** teacher;   **6.** meeting;
7. worry; Hidden word: Spencer.

Chapters 5–7

A:
In order: 3, 1, 4, 2, 7, 5, 6

B:
1. T;   **2.** T;   **3.** F;   **4.** T;   **5.** F;   **6.** T.

C:
1. scared;   **2.** actually;   **3.** nervous;   **4.** flying;   **5.** crying;   **6.** guess;
7. bones;   **8.** sad.

D:
1. business;   **2.** boyfriend;   **3.** bag;   **4.** believe;   **5.** baby;   **6.** bones;
7. broken.

Background Reading:

Spotlight on . . . *City Life and Country Life*

A. Read about James and Maggie Price and answer the questions below.

From City to Country

Many people are growing tired of city life and moving out to the country. Banker James Price and his wife, Maggie, manager of a central London music store, are just two of many who are giving up good jobs and expensive houses for a simpler, quieter life.

Price, 29, says, "City life is just too much. I work for a large bank six, sometimes seven, days a week. I want to see my wife more often. I want to start a family and watch my children grow up somewhere pleasant—not in a dirty noisy city."

The Prices are selling their £1 million flat in south London and moving to Thwaite, a very small village in North Yorkshire.

"I don't know what we'll do for work when we get there," says Maggie Price, 27. "But I'm sure we'll find something. We've bought a nice house with a large piece of land so we can grow our own fruit and vegetables. And I'm a music teacher so I'm sure I can find something to do. Really, I'm just looking forward to a nice quiet life."

1. How do you think the Prices' lives will change when they move to the country?

2. What will the other people in the village of Thwaite think of the Prices when they move there?

3. Where do you think it will be better for the Prices' children to grow up? Why?

B. Read the article and answer the questions below.

Thinking of moving to the country —five things to think about!

1. Don't move to the country because it looks beautiful in the summer. Find out what it's like in the winter: cold, wet, dark . . . ?

2. Don't think life will be the same in the country as in the city. It won't. It will be very different. Imagine you are moving to a foreign country.

3. Make sure you know what to expect. If you need takeout pizzas, weekly trips to the cinema, and a fast Internet service, you could become unhappy very quickly.

4. Don't choose a place to move to after just one visit. Make sure you know what it's like at different times of year—summer, winter, holiday weekends; and different times of day—there may be a lot of cars around at certain times of day.

5. Don't think you will be different in the country. If you sit and watch TV all day in the city, you'll probably do it in the country, too.

1. Which of the above ideas do you think is the most important? Why?

2. Do any of the ideas above surprise you? Which?

3. Can you think of other things to tell people who are thinking of moving to the country?

Background Reading:

Spotlight on . . . *Ghosts*

A. Read the newspaper article and answer the questions below.

The Ghost Bus

"I came round the corner and this bus was coming fast towards me," Bill Masters told the police. "The lights were on but there was nobody on the bus at all. It was coming towards me so fast, I had to drive off the road. My car hit the front of a shop and just missed a woman and her children."

Bill Masters could have been dreaming or imagining things when this happened. But he wasn't alone. Hundreds of other car users in the 1930s had bad experiences with the "ghost bus" in the North Kensington area of London—always along the same stretch of road.

After one accident, when a man died, many people told police that they saw the ghost bus at the time.

There were many more accidents until finally people decided it would be a good idea to make some changes to the road. After that, there were fewer accidents and no one ever saw the ghost bus again.

1. Do you think people really saw a ghost bus?

2. If not, what do you think they saw?

3. Why do you think so many people saw it?

4. Why do you think no one saw the bus after the road changed?

B. Read the interview and answer the questions on the following page.

Ghost Hunter

Our reporter, Jane Gaskell, talks to Brian Seaton, the man who knows more about ghosts than most other people in Britain. The interview takes place in Green Park in Central London.

JG: Obviously people know about you through your books about ghosts. And in fact there is a place very close to here where people sometimes see a ghost.

BS: That's true. Just over to our right there is a strange tree. It's called Dead Man's tree. In about 1820 there was a young man whose wife and four children died in a house fire. He was so unhappy that he shot himself and died under the tree.

JG: And it is his ghost that you can see.

BS: That's right. On dark nights people have seen a tall, thin figure standing near the tree.

JG: Have you ever seen his ghost?

BS: No I haven't. But I have visited the tree. It has a strange air to it. Children don't play near it; dogs don't go near it; people just seem to keep away from it. And I met a lady last year who spends a lot of time in the park. She told me she saw the ghost a couple of years ago on Christmas Eve.

JG: Amazing! Now then, tell me: how did you first become interested in looking for ghosts?

BS: Well, . . .

1. Are there any places near where you live where people believe there are ghosts? Where?

2. Do you believe that ghosts exist or not? If not, why not? If so, what do you think they are?

3. Do you know any good ghost stories? What are they about?

Glossary

afraid	(*adj.*) having a feeling of fear
annoyed	(*adj.*) slightly angry
DNA	(*n.*) a chemical in the cells of all living things that contains genetic information
ghost	(*n.*) the spirit of a dead person
lock	(*n.*) to close something so that only a key will open it
scared	(*adj.*) having a feeling of fear
terrible	(*adj.*) very bad
tidy	(*adj.*) neat, everything in its correct place